U.S. JOB SEARCH SUCCESS FOR INTERNATIONAL STUDENTS

How to Network Like an American

Judy Shen-Filerman
Harvard MBA, Career Expert

For my immigrant parents,

who exercised heroism everyday,

by the simple gesture of making conversation

with their American neighbors and co-workers.

My admiration for their courage to face their vulnerabilities

by engaging in everyday conversations, as awkward as they felt,

in order to feel a sense of belonging in their place of work

and in their new home, America.

Table of Contents

Foreword

Congratulations!

I'm so glad you're reading this book! It's a sign that you want to succeed in the United States – and you will!

Coming to the United States when I was 6 and watching my parents learn to adapt to the American culture has given me a unique experience. I have come to understand that culture plays a huge part in your everyday life: how comfortable you feel ordering a meal at a restaurant…asking for something from a professor…making friends with an American.

If you're new to the United States, there will be amazingly wonderful times — meeting new people and enjoying new experiences! But there will also be times when you feel like you are struggling to understand how things work in this new place.

I've written this book because I know just how hard job search networking is for international students. For the last 10 years, having met thousands of students, I know how "weird" the U.S. job search process is for many international students. What exactly do I do? Is it really okay to email strangers? What do I say when I meet them? How do I write my introductory emails? How do I stay in touch? So many questions!

As a career coach, I've created this book so it's easy to read, with lots of examples. You'll even see my picture pop up throughout to give you encouragement or special comments. It'll be as if I'm doing this with you!

Networking in a new culture takes a lot of courage — and practice! You can do it! Turn the page and let's get started.

Introduction

What Is Networking?

Networking is developing relationships with acquaintances and strangers that allow you to learn about careers, while opening doors to job opportunities. Also, students in the U.S. are allowed, and even encouraged, to contact more senior level individuals to seek advice. While this practice is forbidden in many cultures around the world, it is how networking is done in the United States. A networking contact may be a speaker who comes to campus, a recent graduate found on LinkedIn, or a referral from a professor. Of course, Americans network with friends and relatives. But there are "rules" for networking in the U.S., so it's very important that you understand the idea well. This book will teach you all you need to know so you can network correctly and effectively, and get the positive results you want.

Why Network?

You probably think that applying for a job online is a great way to find work. With so much done online, who wouldn't think that! But believe it or not, applying online is not an effective way to get a job. In fact, 70% of jobs in the United States are found through networking. This means that networking is the most effective method to use when searching for work. That is why it is so important that you know how to network the right way.

Having coached thousands of international students over the last decade, I know that many believe high grades will get them a job in the U.S. But this is simply not true. High grades are helpful, but they will not make a person stand out. International students must understand what it really takes to get a job in the U.S. Frankly, most international students do well with their technical grades, but what makes a person stand out is how he or she communicates. Employers care more about this than grades. The big question employers ask is: "Can this student work well in the United States, and work well with other Americans?" To answer their question, you will need to prove your interpersonal and communications skills! These skills shine through when you network.

I'm so glad you are reading this book. Networking is critical if you want to find a job in the U.S. Although acquiring this skill is important for Americans, it is even more important for international students to master it. Networking is one of the only ways you are able to showcase

your interpersonal communications skills and professional capabilitie
to people who can help you develop, get an interview, or get hired for
a job.

Can International Students Network Well Enough to Get a Job?

Of course they can! I've known many students who have found
incredible jobs through networking. However, students must be
willing to use methods that are different from what they are used to.
Networking requires students to work hard in areas that have nothing
to do with "book smarts." How you speak, how you tell stories, how
you use language to persuade others…these are the skills needed
for effective networking. Most of all, networking requires a time
commitment, practice, and asking for feedback. The most successful
students have been those who are willing to commit the time and put
in the effort needed to network. There is no shortcut to success.

How to Get the Most Out of This Book

A GUIDELINES / INSTRUCTIONS

Examples:

- How to start your emails.
- What language to use in opening paragraphs.
- How soon should you contact someone if they don't respond to your email?
- How to carry on a networking conversation.
- How to stay in touch after you've met.

This section gives overall strategies for a particular networking-related activity.

B CULTURAL CUES

Examples:

- Don't start opening paragraphs with "It's of the greatest honor that I am contacting you." Use a more equal tone, "I'm very excited to learn about you through the alumni office."
- When you meet your contact, initiate small talk to show friendliness and professionalism. Americans don't feel comfortable with a long stretch of silence.
- Handshakes should be firm, regardless of whether you are a woman or a man.

This section gives important U.S. cultural norms to be aware of in your networking practice.

This section gives actual examples of written/spoken language used in job search networking.

C   CASE STUDY / LANGUAGE EXAMPLES

Sample Email

Subject Line: American Business University Student Seeking Your Counsel

Thursday, Nov. 29, 2015

Dear Ms. Riley,

My name is Arjun Gupta and I'm pursuing a Masters of Finance at American Business University. I am contacting you to learn more about career development in corporate finance. I learned about you through the alumni office and have been very impressed by your career accomplishments.

Prior to this, I was a manufacturing engineer at ABC Bottling Company. I've always enjoyed using my strong quantitative and analytical knowledge to model and design manufacturing lines. Also satisfying was working with my team to turn models into a practical reality. Today, I hope to apply my interest in quants and modeling to financial modeling. I'm excited about equity financial analysis because of its complexity. I look forward to the opportunity to use analytical modeling to better understand the underlying dynamics that are driving share price.

I hope to have an opportunity to speak with you in the next couple of weeks, at a time most convenient for you. Thank you in advance for your consideration.

Sincerely,

Arjun Gupta

The 3 Critical Phases: The "Musts" for Success!

Most students just want to get out there and network! They want a job and they want it now! They say, "Get me to a career fair! I just need to pass out more business cards! This will work!" Well, I hate to be the one to tell you this, but this is not going to work. There are three critical phases and each needs to be completed by you. That is what will work!

1) Understanding Networking

You must know why and how Americans network, so you know what we expect. Only then will you know what you need to do to be successful.

2) Preparing for Networking

Most students dislike preparing for networking, and that is why they have poor results. With a little effort and planning, you can set yourself up to network successfully and find that job you are looking for.

Do you know what makes you a strong candidate for a job? No, it's not your good grades. It's your interpersonal communications skills.

Do you have a personal story that will help others understand why you are the right person for a job? Can you can tell this story with ease and confidence?

Do you know anything about your contact? What will you say that he or she will find appealing? How can you connect with that person in a way that will make you stand out?

Do you know how to ask for a job without actually asking for the job? Knowing how to do this is a true skill and proper American etiquette.

You may feel so nervous that you can't even start. "I'll be so embarrassed. I've never done this before." It's okay to feel that way. Most Americans also hate to network, but we do it anyway because we have to. Take it one step at a time. How about just going to a workshop to learn more?

3) Doing Networking

Practice is the key to success! There's no better time than now! Do any of these excuses sound familiar?

- "I don't want to practice because I'm too busy with school work." Well, then I guess you really don't want a job. You've got to practice networking to get good at it, and networking is the best way to find a job.
- "I feel embarrassed practicing." Well, it's better to be embarrassed now than when it really matters. No one is born a master networker. We all have to practice and you are no different. Have fun with it!
- "I don't feel I do it right and so I don't feel ready." Don't worry. Like anything else, the more you practice, the better you'll become. Give it a try and you'll see.

Remember, networking has nothing to do with how smart you are. It's about courage, taking risks, and taking action. It's also about taking control of your professional future. It's like swimming. You can't read a book on swimming and expect to jump into the pool and swim perfectly. You might struggle at first. It might feel a little scary, too. That's normal. You need to be brave and practice with advisors and classmates. The more you practice, the better the swimmer you become. It's like that with networking, too. Regular practice is the only way you'll get better at it.

Understanding Networking

CHAPTER OUTLINE

1) Why Networking is an Imperative for the U.S. Job Search

2) What is Networking Like in the United States?

3) Networking is Absolutely Possible for International Students

4) Success Stories

5) Key Success Factors

Networking opens the door for international students. It is the most critical job search channel for international students because:

American employers want to know you. Your resume and grades can only say so much, and they do not help you stand out, especially when compared to American applicants also applying for a job.

When Americans get to know you personally, they feel it's less of a risk hiring a non-American. You've shown that you can fit into the culture of an American organization.

Networking leads to…

Internal Advocates / Unadvertised jobs

Visa Sponsorship / Cost

Fear of rejection is the major reason many students don't ever network. That totally makes sense! I've been rejected when networking. It hurts and can feel embarrassing. But I knew — if networking will help me achieve my goals, then I need to feel uncomfortable to get where I want to be. With practice, I got better at it. And you will, too. I've always admired the students who were courageous enough to make contact with strangers in a new culture. Forget about the results — just taking the first step is an act of bravery that you need to celebrate!

1) Why Networking is an Imperative for the U.S. Job Search

In the U.S., 70% of jobs are found through networking! As I explained earlier, the most effective way to get a job in the U.S. is through networking — not by applying for a job online. Many apply for jobs online, but no one really stands out. It may take more effort, but the return on your time investment is much higher when you network. If you're not networking, you're losing a major source of possible new jobs!

2) What is Networking like in the U.S.?

Unlike many other cultures, Americans network with people they know and don't know. In addition, in the U.S., students are allowed — even encouraged — to contact more senior level individuals to seek advice. This practice may be forbidden in many cultures around the world, but in the U.S. it is accepted and a way of life. A networking contact may be a speaker who comes on campus, a recent graduate found on LinkedIn, or a referral from a professor. Of course, it's also helpful to network with friends and relatives. However, just like all cultures, the U.S. has "rules" for networking. It's very important that you understand these rules well. This will help you navigate the process effectively and get positive results.

3) Networking is Absolutely Possible for International Students

Having worked with thousands of students, I can guarantee you that international students can be successful at networking. The majority of the students I have coached who found jobs in the U.S., got their jobs through networking. It is a process that has proven results!

4) Success Stories

Joy was a Chinese student pursuing her Masters in Marketing Analytics. She truly enjoyed this work but was quite shy and did not like to network with the crowds at career fairs. But because she did well academically, she started to help her professor, and in so doing, he realized how talented she was. In an unusual move, he recommended Joy to his friend who owned a marketing analytics company. Joy performed so well during the internship that she was offered a full-time job for which the owner sponsored her H1B visa. What we learn through Joy's story is that networking is not always at the career fair or with on-campus recruiters. If you are outstanding at what you do and

thers find out through working with you, you've networked, but in a
much more indirect way.

) Key Success Factors

Understand what we Americans expect. Learn to look through our *cultural lens.*

Expect to be uncomfortable. Change is uncomfortable but know you'll be okay.

Learn the U.S. networking protocols. What you should and should not do.

Make sure you're prepared with good research on contacts and industry.

Get advice from your career management advisors, more experienced students, and recent alumni who have successfully networked for a job.

Practice, practice, practice. Get feedback. Doing it is the only way to improve.

Know you will be scared. Know you may feel rejected. But be brave enough to do it anyway.

Preparing for Networking: Part One

If you want to succeed in networking, preparation can make the difference between success and failure! Take the necessary time to create a persuasive career story that connects you with your networking contact, which means you must research your contact's experience, interests, etc. Follow the 7 steps outlined in this chapter to prepare for successful networking.

1) Your Objectives

Break down your goals into two groups:

A. Your job search objectives

By pre-defining your objectives, you'll make the best decisions every step of the way. What kind of work in the U.S. will really benefit you?

- What type of work are you looking for?
- What is the actual position you will be happy with?
- What characteristics of a company will suit you best? In other words, which industry do you wish to work in? What size company are you looking for?

- What do you *want to gain or learn* from this experience?
  How long do you want to work in the U.S.?
  - Conduct a dual search back at home or a non-U.S. location to increase your success rate.
- If not the U.S., what is your other search plan?

As I've already said, preparation is so important. But it takes time and it requires perseverance to do things you have not done in the past. Many international students have never had to create a personal story to tell others. Most have never had to research a job or an industry. Moreover, most students are unsure where to find contacts or why they need to research about their networking contacts. So much of this is new. So many international students wonder why it's necessary. I always say it's like dating. Would you date someone who had no idea who you were or didn't care what you were interested in? Never. Networking is no different. Your networking contact wants to know that you invested your time to learn about them, their work, and their company.

For you to be successful in networking in the U.S., you must see through the American lens. We value individualism, independent thinking, and the personal expression of ideas. Many community-oriented cultures value the larger group more than the individual and find the personal expression of thought rude or selfish. But please remember — this is not how we see it in the U.S. When you do not express yourself, Americans do not see that as humble, we simply think you lack ideas, passion, and interest.

II. Your networking objectives

Networking can be utilized for different reasons:

Learning

Often called "informational interviews," these networking meetings usually occur when you first start school and are trying to get information about a job or industry you're interested in. Or you may want to learn from others how their careers developed. Informational interviews are very useful not only for learning, but also for establishing relationships with people who may assist you in getting interviews in the future.

Asking

As you get into your second semester, or when it is almost time to start interviewing for your internship or full-time job, you can reconnect with the people you spoke with during your informational interviews. It's wise to choose the people you think have a very positive impression of you. This is the time when it is within protocol — or acceptable — to ask these people for job contacts or possible openings in their company. However, how you ask is very important. Get suggestions from your Career Office or from experienced students on how to word this correctly.

2) Developing Your General Career Story

In America, we expect job search candidates to showcase or demonstrate their unique talents and skills. We want to hear how they are a match to a position or industry. Basically, we want the person looking for the job to answer, "Why should I hire you?" Be sure you are ready to answer that question.

We expect a person to be an effective and eloquent storyteller. We expect a person to be able to talk about themselves in a positive way to others. This may be a new behavior for many non-Americans, but it is normal in U.S. culture.

Americans believe that if a person can effectively tell a story about themselves and persuade how we view them, that they will be effective and persuasive in the workplace. This is a skill Americans value highly.

U.S. Value	Characteristic
Individualism	Uniqueness/Passion
Equality Rights	Owns a Point of View
Self-Made	Overcome/Achieve/Lead
Fact-Based Proof	Proven Skills
Transaction-Based Relationships	Spotlight Socializing

Telling Your Unique and Relevant Story

Networking contacts want to understand the "whole" you so they can assess:

- Your skills and talent. Are your skills transferrable to the industry or job?
- Your true interest and passion. (Remember: Strong grades are not enough!)
- Your interpersonal and communications skills.
- Your cultural and organizational fit.

Your Cultural and Organizational Fit

Expressing Your Personality

American recruiters often comment that international students seem "robotic," which reflects their need to see the "authentic" you. Your personality is very important to recruiters. What does that mean, many of you may ask. Which adjectives would describe the authentic you while also addressing the needs of employers? Words such as innovative, detailed, creative, collaborative, optimistic, and determined are good examples.

Take the time to reflect back on your life and determine charateristics that have helped you be successful. Be ready to have examples that demonstrate the situations where your personality helped you succeed.

Along with defining your personality, you also need to express your:

<u>Purpose</u>: a lifelong goal you have, that would give your life meaning and fulfillment (which is reflected in your career choice).

<u>Passion</u>: a deep interest that you feel you must pursue in your life.

Your General Career Story Must Meet *Employer* Needs: Must-Haves in Your General Career Story

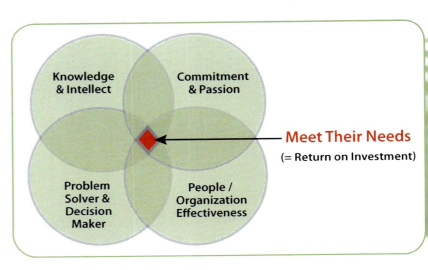

Knowledge and Intellect: Your story must explain your technical knowledge, your grades, and your practical experience.

Commitment and Passion: Your story must reflect your proven interest and curiosity about the job, industry, or field of work.

Problem Solver and Decision Maker: Your story must show your ability to identify and solve problems. Show that you go above and beyond simply finishing the tasks sent your way!

People and Organizational Effectiveness: Your story must showcase your ability to communicate clearly. Make them see that you can successfully collaborate with your American peers and managers.

Follow these tips to prepare the most effective career story to use while networking.

Expandable: Have both a 30-second "pitch" and a longer story ready. The pitch describes your talents, strengths, or why someone should hire you. The longer story should provide "proof" to support the claims you made in your pitch.

Address Employer's Top Needs: Your career story should reflect the research you have done on the industry, prospective employers, and your networking contact. Your story should match their top interests and needs.

Proven: Your story should include "mini-stories" that show your interests, talents, and skills.

Clearly Communicated: Tell your story in a logical, easy-to-understand, and interesting way. Do not just give a "list" of things you've done.

Personally Unique: Make sure your story is truly your own and unique. It should not sound like anyone else's story. Your story is your moment to shine!

I've found that many international students, especially those from Asia, find it difficult to understand why managers would want "independent thinkers" who will speak up and give their ideas, even if it disagrees with their superiors. This is a very challenging concept to grasp for some because many cultures are much more hierarchical. However, it is vital that you can show you are creative and able to identify issues and opportunities, beyond being good at "doing things that are given to you."

Preparing for Networking: Part Two

CHAPTER OUTLINE

1) Target Job Positions

When you talk to your networking contact, they'll want to know what kind of jobs you are interested in. It will be very unproductive for you if you are too general and fail to show specific interest in a certain position or two. You don't have to choose only one job, but it will help if you describe certain kinds of jobs that utilize skills you are learning in school. In fact, networking contacts may not respond to you if they think you are unfocused.

Consider your degree or area of specialization. What are the types of jobs most graduates seek? If you are unsure how to answer this question, you can get this information from your career management office. Advisors are usually a great source of information, as they have worked with many students just like you, in the past.

Research resources such as The Vault, Wet Feet Guide, and The Bureau of Labor Statistics to get a more detailed understanding of related jobs.

Details you should know:

> Job titles

> Job responsibilities

> Outputs

> Strategic roles in an organization

> Compensation

Understandably, many newly arrived students who have little / no work experience tend to have no idea what types of jobs they should target. I would strongly recommend that you speak with your career management advisor or academic advisor, so they can give you some suggestions of jobs to explore. It is very hard for you to know at the outset. Once you've gotten some suggestions, read the job descriptions and determine if this is something that you are interested in and if you have skills that are proven and/or related.

2) Research the Industry

Knowing the kind of jobs that interest you is very important. But it's also important for you to understand the industry that these jobs are a part of. You will impress your networking contacts when you show that you've taken the time to research trends in their company, their industry, and their competitors. If you haven't researched this information, it will be obvious and your networking contact might assume you are not truly interested in the job. The depth of knowledge you possess reflects how much you really want employment.

Here are some details you should gather as you research your chosen industry:

Industry Search

- Context
  - › Industry or sub-industry trends
  - › Key issues

- Company
  - › Mission, key goals
  - › Key businesses / business units
  - › Global reach
  - › Critical business drivers
  - › Performance
  - › Who's in management — their professional/personal background

- Customers
  - › Key customers (buyers, users)
  - › Needs
  - › Geography

- Channel
  - › Key paths to deliver products or services

- Competitors
  - › Key competitors
  - › Comparisons on key measures

Where to Find Information

There are two types of sources to research information on positions, companies, and industries: Primary and secondary.

Primary sources are people. Who are they?

- Professionals working in the field (e.g. your alumni)
- Recruiters
- Professors
- Classmates

Secondary resources are reports. For example:

- Search engine results (e.g. from Google)
- Databases (e.g. The Vault or Bloomberg)
- Magazines / newspapers
- Blogs
- Research papers

Typically, primary sources provide more in-depth, non-publicized information. For example, the culture of an organization or career development path. Therefore, your research will be most effective if you first conduct secondary research and then utilize primary research to gain in-depth information you wouldn't find in secondary sources. Primary sources can provide very important details for your industry/company/job choice. That's why informational interviews in networking are so helpful to job seekers.

3) Find and Research Networking Contacts

Find Networking Contacts

Networking contacts can be found from many sources, including primary sources (direct experiences you've had) and secondary sources (gained through media or social networks).

Primary Sources

- American classmates
- Professors
- Alumni
- Professional Associations
- Cultural Associations
- Speakers

Secondary Sources

- Alumni directory
- LinkedIn

One of the biggest complaints I hear from international students who have just arrived in the U.S. is their belief that they do not know anyone. While it is true they know fewer people than a person who has lived in the U.S. for many years, it's actually very easy to connect to people in the United States. One of the most useful sources for networking contacts is your university alumni. The university alumni system is often used by people searching for a job, so take advantage of it, too! Search for alumni in LinkedIn, for starters. Join related online discussion groups. Don't be afraid to get out there and introduce yourself online.

- Facebook
- Google
- Industry databases
- Conference websites

Research Networking Contacts

When you meet with your networking contact, you want to show you've taken the time to research and understand their professional background and interests. The information you gather will help you in two ways: You will have data points to use during your conversation, and you will know what specific questions to ask when you meet.

Here are some details you should gather as you research your networking contact:

- Educational degrees and majors.
- Geography of their studies.
- Their career path: positions, responsibilities, companies, industries.
- Articles or blogs they've written.

Think ahead to prepare yourself for conversation topics by analyzing your research:

- What does the contact's career path tell you about his / her passions and interests?
- What skills and experiences does a strong candidate possess?
- How do they feel about career switchers?
- What strong points of view do they hold about this industry?
- How would they want to help you?

Sources:

- LinkedIn
- Google
- Bloomberg
- Functional Publications (e.g. finance, marketing, etc).
- Ask your career management office for other sources.

4) Develop Your Targeted Career Story

Once you've narrowed your search to a particular job and company you should then create a targeted career story that shows your contact you have specific interest in his/her company. The more your career story matches the job's needs and the situation of your networking contact, the more they will take you seriously and take the extra steps to help you.

The examples below show you the power of a targeted career story. **If you were a networking contact, which story would interest you more?**

BEFORE: A GENERAL CAREER STORY

I am currently pursuing a Masters in Finance at American Business University. I'm very interested in developing my career in investment management.

Before business school, I was a manufacturing engineer where I worked in the bottling plant for a bottle manufacturer. I am very quantitative and analytical. I have been very strong in my mathematics and in creating mathematical models. I am a very hardworking person. I think investment management requires people who are able to commit themselves to the work.

I hope to apply my strong analytical skills to the area of investment management.

AFTER RESEARCHING: A TARGETED CAREER STORY

I am currently pursuing a Masters in Finance at American Business University. I'm very interested in developing my career in investment management and I've been fascinated by your CIO's recent change in investment strategies.

Prior to my studies, I was a manufacturing process engineer, with a strong quantitative and analytical background. I've enjoyed analyzing complex data and making sense of them, such as working with my team when the plant had major crises. Being from an emerging market like India, I understand first-hand the interplay between macroeconomics, local investments, regulations, and trade. I thrive in fast-paced environments and have always focused on working with others to solve problems and create solutions. The emerging markets are very dynamic, and I look forward to the opportunity to help your firm maximize its market performance.

While international students often tell me that Americans are great storytellers and they can't compare, I often remind them that every culture has great storytellers. The difference in the U.S. is that we expect *everyone* to have a story, while in some cultures, only certain persons (males, senior levels) are permitted to tell stories in public. Americans *want* to hear your story. We love stories. So don't ever feel like you are being rude. In fact, the more stories you can tell, the better your connection with Americans!

5) Tell Your Career Story

Your story will appeal to your networking contact if it is:

- Personalized
- Told around a key point that is easy to grasp
- Relates easily to him/her
- Shows your competence, knowledge of the industry and genuine interest

Telling your story in an effective way is critical. Great storytellers:

1. Practice and practice until it feels natural to tell the story.
2. Feel their story (different from memorizing the story).
3. Know the most important points.
4. Are expressive, personable and engaging.

Doing Networking

Doing networking isn't about being smart. Doing networking is about being brave, courageous and persistent in the face of rejection and discomfort. It's also about taking action that would have seemed "socially rude" in some cultures. "I couldn't possibly contact a senior recruiter in my home country. That would be simply unacceptable." Yes, you are right about your home country, but the United States is very different. We have different rules and expectations. Going out to network in a new country, like the U.S., is not easy, but many students have done it successfully. It is most important to be willing to take risks and make mistakes. There will be people who never answer your emails or calls. You will face rejection. However, try your best to not take it personally. Remember, you may get one hundred "No's" but all you need is one "Yes!" Some of the most successful literary works (Harry Potter for example) were turned down many, many times before they were finally published!

) How to Introduce Yourself to Your Networking Contact

For most international students, "doing" networking is the most frightening part of the job search process. It's totally understandable. You've prepared and researched. You've created your story. Now you need to make contact with an alumnus but you're not quite sure how to go about it: *What do I say? How do I say it? Do I call or email? What do I say during my 30-minute conversation? What is and isn't allowed? What if I make a mistake?*

Preparing thoroughly will help you feel much more confident when you are ready to "do" networking. If you've never done networking before, it is so important that you practice and get feedback. *Networking is not a natural thing we do*, so you'll need to practice telling your story, get feedback on the appropriateness of your emails, and engage in mock networking conversations so you can get used to the typical flow of conversation. Even though our networking methods seem vague, there is a process you'll need to follow, so it's important that you understand it!

Be very careful how you address your networking contact and what you write. Americans have clear expectations on the wording and structure of introductory emails, so please make sure you get feedback, in addition to referring to the sample we provide.

You must make sure there are no misspellings or incorrect grammar! Americans will judge your professionalism and attention to detail here. It is absolutely in your control to make sure your writing, cover letter, and resume are perfect, so please be thorough and detailed in your proofreading.

Introduction: 3 Steps

1. Creating your email
2. Sending your email
3. Following-up if you don't get a reply

1. Creating Your Email

A   GUIDELINES / INSTRUCTIONS

- Make sure your contact will open your email. Remember — she or he doesn't know you and your email could be perceived as spam. This is why your subject line is critical. You should refer to the school such as "University MBA student seeking your counsel" or "Referred to you by University Alumni Office."

- Your email should have 3 main paragraphs:

  > Paragraph 1 Who you are, how you were referred (a "safe" connection), why you want to speak with this person.

  > Paragraph 2 Your Core Story, modified to this particular opportunity. Highlight your most relevant key selling points, and connect them to this area of work. Show your genuine interest and passion for this area of work or your curiosity about how it works.

  > Paragraph 3 Closing. Communicate your excitement to meet with the person. Provide a time period, between 2 weeks and 1 month, during which you would like to meet.

B   CULTURAL CUES

DO...

- Use your alumni connections as this is one of the most powerful networks in the U.S.. Alumni usually feel connected to their alma mater and feel obliged to support current university students. Thus, writing the university connection in the email subject line is critical.

- Discuss your passions and interests as they connect to the industry or position. Networking contacts want to know who you are, not just about your competencies. This is an effective way to create a personal connection.

- Choose one or two key selling points. Stay focused on what's most relevant.

DON'T...

- Start your email with highly honorable verbiage such as, "It is with the greatest honor that I have this opportunity to connect with you." We see such show of respect as overdoing it and it makes us uncomfortable.

- Get too informal. Always start with "Dear _____," not "Hi there." Use words like "your group," not "you guys." Americans are informal but there is a business formality in communications that can be confusing to international students.

- Create a "list" of skills. That will be evident in your resume. Highlight key aspects and make connections to this person's interests.

Your subject line should encourage them to open the email!

Explain who you are; you are a "safe" connection.

Your Core Story; similar to your 30-second pitch.

Set a time when you would like to follow up.

Make sure you begin and end emails with standard greetings!

C CASE STUDY / LANGUAGE EXAMPLES

Sample Email

Subject Line: University of America Business School Student Seeking Your Counsel

Dear Ms. Riley,

My name is Arjun Gupta and I'm pursuing an MBA degree at University of America Business School. I am contacting you to learn more about career development in corporate finance. I learned about you through the alumni office and have been very impressed by your career accomplishments. I hope to have the opportunity to speak with you to learn more about your career path and to gain your counsel as I consider entering your field of work.

Prior to this, I was a manufacturing engineer at ABC Bottling Company. I always enjoyed using my strong quantitative and analytical knowledge to model and design manufacturing lines. Also satisfying was working with my team to turn the model into a practical reality. Today, I hope to apply my interest in quants and modeling to financial modeling. I'm particularly interested in corporate finance because of its critical role in enabling companies to decide on projects that affect a company's revenue, profitability, and success. Such a position would also give me an opportunity to work with people across functions, which I have always enjoyed.

I hope to have an opportunity to speak with you in the next couple of weeks, at a time most convenient for you. Thank you in advance for your consideration.

Sincerely,

Arjun Gupta

Sending Your Email

A   GUIDELINES / INSTRUCTIONS

- Check to make sure spelling and grammar are correct. Get an American friend or your advisor to review it first. Spelling mistakes indicate a lack of attention to detail. Grammar mistakes may cause English fluency concerns with your networking contact.
- Send your email at the beginning of the day when your contact is more likely to check it. In the middle of the day, most people are checking for "must" emails and may pass on opening your email.
- Send emails individually, even if the contacts are in the same organization. Don't send "group" emails. You want to personalize each email contact.

B   CULTURAL CUES

DO...

- Send emails to work email addresses.

DON'T...

- Send emails to private emails addresses unless you've been given an introduction or you know that it is the preferred address to use.
- Send emails on weekends if this is your first time making contact, as most Americans see weekends as "private" time.

It is helpful to understand that Americans are protective of "private" information. Therefore, new contacts, like you, should use only *work* emails and phone numbers. Never initiate contact with private contact information, including mobile numbers unless you have confirmation from the contact.

Alerting Your Contact of Your Email with a Phone Call

A   GUIDELINES / INSTRUCTIONS

- It's within etiquette to get your networking contact to notice your email by prompting them with a call.
- Call to let him/her know you've sent an email and why you sent the email.
- If you prefer to not speak with him/her, you can leave a voice mail very early in the day or late in the evening, when you think the person may not be there.
- Be ready to speak with them live should they pick up. Don't hang up. Remember, your objective is to talk to him/her!

B   CULTURAL CUES

DO...

- Call your contact directly to follow up on a request for a meeting. This is an acceptable practice in the U.S. If your contact is a C-suite level executive, your call will likely be routed to his/her assistant. If so, work with the assistant to set up a meeting.
- Call with excitement and confidence. Let your voice express that you are a confident and engaged professional (smiling as you talk helps!). Practice, practice, practice to make sure your voice is professional and confident.
- Spend a few minutes talking to your contact should he/she pick up. This is the time to share your Career Story. Help them get to know you. Ask if they have time to talk and then make sure you try to secure a meeting time with them.

DON'T...

- Be too informal or too formal. Your natural personality will help you to connect with your networking contact. But the person is not your friend, so do not use slang in these conversations.
- Take up too much time should your contact pick up. They were not expecting your call. Ask if they have time to talk or if you can set up a time, while you're on the phone with them.

C   CASE STUDY / LANGUAGE EXAMPLES

Sample Phone Call or Voice Mail Message

Good Morning / Afternoon / Evening, Ms. Riley,

My name is (*your name*). I received your name and contact information from the alumni office at my university or business school program.

I just sent an email to you yesterday, in the hopes of meeting with you to learn more about your career development in (*industry, company*). I was very excited to learn about your (*something about them that particularly excited you*).

Is this a good time for a conversation or should I set up for another time?

I look forward to having the opportunity to speak with you for 30-45 minutes at a time most convenient for you.

Thank you for your time, Ms. Riley. I look forward to speaking with you at greater length at another time.

How and when to follow up after emails are sent is very confusing to students. We ask students to "be assertive but not pushy." What does that mean, exactly?

Basically, it's okay to follow up weekly for a month, but then you need to give your contact space and not be a "stalker." If you're in doubt, ask your advisor!

3. Following Up If You Don't Get a Reply

A   GUIDELINES / INSTRUCTIONS

- It's within networking protocol to call or email within 5-7 days, if you don't hear back from the contact.
- If you follow up with an email, it's best to forward the original email so they can refer to it and you can prove you did send an email.
- Remember, the person you sent your email to may not even have received it. Some emails may go directly to "junk mail" on email accounts or considered spam.
- Assume that the person did not receive your email and use a tone in your email that is patient and professional.
- This email should be shorter — do not give too much background about yourself, which you did in your first email.

B   CULTURAL CUES

- Following up shows your interest and commitment. Americans do not view this as being too pushy or rude. Many networking contacts are very busy and even if they did read your email, they may not have had time to respond to you.
- It is important that you are professional in your follow-up. It's a good idea to recognize "how busy they are" and appreciate them taking the time to meet with you. Then you can go directly to asking for an opportunity to meet.
- Never express impatience, as it is a sign of being unprofessional and may cause your contact to dismiss you entirely.

ollow Up Email

Sample Follow-Up Email (one week after the initial contact)

December 6, 2015

Dear Ms. Riley,

Good morning or Good afternoon. My name is _____. I am currently a student at _____. I was referred to you by _____ (*alumni office, professor, etc.*). I sent you an email on Thursday, Nov. 29th inquiring about setting up a meeting to learn more about your career. I was hoping to meet with you when you are available. I understand how busy you must be, and I would very much appreciate if we could find a time to meet.

Restate some of your experiences, but make this email more direct and shorter.

I hope to have an opportunity to meet with you in the next couple of weeks when it is convenient for you. I can be reached at this email address. Thank you very much in advance for your consideration.

Sincerely,

Arjun Gupta

Calling Back Within 3-7 Days, If You Don't Hear Back from the Contact

C | **CASE STUDY / LANGUAGE EXAMPLES**

Sample Phone Conversations

1. Calling back and leaving a message

Good morning or Good afternoon. My name is (*say your name slowly*). I am currently a student at _____. I was referred to you by _____ (*alumni office, professor, etc.*). I sent you an email on Thursday, Nov. 29th inquiring about setting up a meeting to learn more about your career. I was hoping to meet with you when you are available. I understand how busy you must be and I would very much appreciate it if we could find a time to meet. I can be reached at this email address or (*say your phone number slowly*). I look forward to meeting you. Thank you very much in advance for your consideration.

2. Calling back and the networking contact answers the phone

Ring...Ring...Ring...

Ms. Riley: Hello.

You: Is this Ms. Riley?

Ms. Riley: Yes, this is she.

You: Good morning /afternoon. My name is (*say your name slowly*). I am currently a student at _____. I was referred to you by _____ (*alumni office, professor, etc.*). I sent you an email on Thursday, Nov. 29th inquiring about setting up a meeting to learn more about your career. I understand how busy you must be and I would very much appreciate if we could find a time to meet.

Ms. Riley: I see. I didn't receive any email. Would you mind resending it? Also, in the meantime, you can contact my assistant, Mary, to see my availability for a meeting.

You: Thank you very much. I will do that.

Ms. Riley: I look forward to meeting you.

You: Thank you for your time and I look forward to speaking with you soon.

C   CASE STUDY / LANGUAGE EXAMPLES

Sample Phone Conversations

3. Assistant answers:

You: Good morning or Good afternoon. This is (*say your name*). May I please speak with Ms. Riley? *[To overcome objection, don't allow for any pauses in between that will give the assistant time to interject.]* I am following up on an email I sent Ms. Riley on November 29th and wanted to see if I could set up a meeting with her.

Assistant: What is the meeting about?

You: We are both from (*name the school*). I know Ms. Riley is busy, but I would like to have a short 30 minute conversation to gain career advice from Ms. Riley.

Assistant: Please give me your email address and I will contact you after discussing this with Ms. Riley.

You: Thank you and by the way, may I have your name, please.

Assistant: I'm Mary.

You: Thank you, Mary. My email address is (*say your email address slowly*).

Assistant: We will be back in touch.

You: Thank you very much for your time.

Calling contacts can be one of the most frightening moments! Trust me, I know! It's natural to be very nervous because you don't know what will happen.

Some tips:

1. Have your script ready.

2. Make sure you've practiced it many times, with different scenarios.

3. Say it a few times right before the call.

4. Imagine the call goes beautifully! Really.

5. Take three deep breaths, smile and call!

2) Meet and Converse with Your Contact

Meeting Options

<u>**Phone**</u>

If you feel comfortable with phone conversations in English, then having a phone meeting with your contact is a good way to ease into the process.

Your voice is the only communication tool in phone calls, so body language and non-verbal cues will be lost when compared to meeting in person. Your English fluency, excitement and personal connection will need to be expressed through voice.

<u>**Skype**</u>

It is helpful to use Skype when schedules don't permit you to meet in person. This allows visual and audio communications which may be more effective than phone calls. You can also see the cultural and non-verbal cues in action, even though you are not in the same room with the person.

<u>**In Person**</u>

The additional benefit of meeting in person is you can see the environment that your contact works in, and each of you can take in both implicit and explicit expressions. Also, you may be introduced to other colleagues of the contact — a benefit you don't get from a phone call or Skype meeting.

Your Dress and Appearance

A   GUIDELINES / INSTRUCTIONS

- "You only have one chance to make a good first impression" is an American saying that's important to consider when meeting your networking contact.
- Your appearance, from head to toe, needs to be at its best. Have a professional haircut, wear a suit that fits well, polish your shoes, bring a leather folio and a professional-looking pen.
- Bring a fresh copy of your resume and business cards.
- If you're going to a start-up / small technology company, call the main number to ask if you should dress business formal or business casual.

B   CULTURAL CUES

Professional dress

- In the United States, it is usual for a man to wear a suit, tie and nice dress shoes for networking, especially at blue chip companies, consulting or financial services firms. For a woman, it is usual to wear a business suit or dress with dress shoes. Dress or skirt length should be just-above-the knees or longer.
- Dress shoes means no sneakers, sandals, flip-flops.
- For models of appropriate dress, watch CNBC or CNN news anchors.
- While start-ups and smaller technology companies have more informal dress, it's important to know what is appropriate for the company.
- If you are unsure, it's always better to overdress than to be underdressed.

Arriving at the Office / Skype Environment

A   GUIDELINES / INSTRUCTIONS

In Person

- It is not acceptable to be late for an appointment. Better to arrive 20–30 minutes early than to be 5 minutes late.
- Take the extra time to:
  - › Check your appearance in the rest room (hair, face, dress, teeth).
  - › Survey the office environment to assess formality, people's interactivity, implicit aspects of the organization's culture.

Via Skype

- Make sure the background is neutral — not too informal / messy / with personal pictures, etc.
- Make sure there is enough lighting.
- Check sound level.

B   CULTURAL CUES

- For business appointments, Americans expect you to be on time, arriving before the actual appointment time. If your appointment is at 11am, it's expected you would arrive and check in with security about 10 minutes before the actual appointment so you can start on time.
- Your contact may run late but you are expected to arrive on time.
- Although not required, you can confirm the appointment the day before with your contact or her assistant.
- If you are Skyping (even if your contact knows you'll be in your home), it's important that you dress as if you were going to be meeting in person, with a neutral background.

Networking Conversation Phases

Every culture has its approach to conversations. American networking conversations can very in length, but generally, they are between 20–60 minutes. For business networking conversations in the United States, there are 4 phases: Engage – Ask – Showcase – End, or "EASE"

EASE

Engage	Ask	See-saw	End
Meet & Greet	Small Talk Opening	Learning Showcasing Asking	Closing
(30 seconds)	(5 minutes)	(20 minutes)	(3 minutes)

ENGAGE — Meet & Greet Conversation Flow

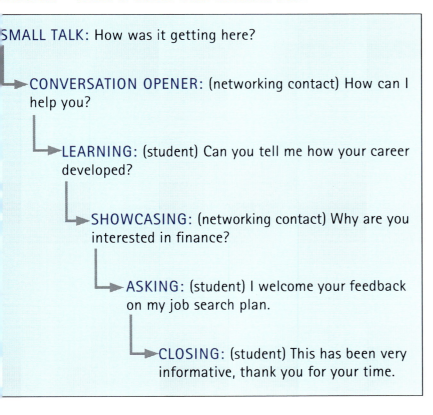

SMALL TALK: How was it getting here?

CONVERSATION OPENER: (networking contact) How can I help you?

LEARNING: (student) Can you tell me how your career developed?

SHOWCASING: (networking contact) Why are you interested in finance?

ASKING: (student) I welcome your feedback on my job search plan.

CLOSING: (student) This has been very informative, thank you for your time.

The networking conversation can be quite complicated for international students because you need to do multiple things at the same time: socialize, sell yourself, listen for cues, and summarize the conversation. It's challenging for Americans to do this! So if you do not have the habit of socializing with older individuals in positions of authority and you are still translating English in your head, navigating a networking conversation can be really challenging. That's why practicing and getting feedback from advisors or American peers is so important. You can't just read about it — do it! You need to experience it and improve it over time. Patience, practice and persistence are key to success.

E–A–S–E Conversation Phases

PHASE 1: ENGAGE

A   GUIDELINES / INSTRUCTIONS

- If you are seated, you are expected to stand up when your networking contact is about 3 steps from you.
- The American handshake is expected between all people in business: men and women, older and younger individuals, senior managers and new hires.
- Immediately after the meet and greet, engage in "small talk" (to be discussed next).

B   CULTURAL CUES

What We Do:

- When you see your networking contact, even if (s)he is a senior manager, Americans do not bow or look away as a sign of respect.
- Because we are a country that believes in social equality, we "engage as equals."
- This means we make eye contact, we smile and provide a firm handshake.
- Professional confidence in the U.S. is defined with a certain body language: standing up straight, being physically open (no crossed arms or shrinking posture), a gentle smile and a firm handshake. This is expected for both men and women.

What We Say:

- Because your networking contact will have read your resume and you will have researched about him/her, your self-introduction is short, unlike the lengthier introduction you would do at a career fair where the recruiter does not know you.

C CASE STUDY / LANGUAGE EXAMPLES

Sample Meet & Greet

> *Ms. Riley walks down the corridor.*
> *When she is 3 steps from Arjun, Arjun stands up.*
> *As she gets within arm's length of Arjun, Arjun makes eye contact and smiles.*

Arjun: Ms. Riley?

Ms. Riley: Yes.

Arjun (extends hand and handshakes)**:** It's very nice to meet you, Ms. Riley. Thank you very much for taking the time to meet with me.

Ms. Riley (extends her hand for handshake)**:** I'm glad to meet you as well, Arjun. Please call me Susan.

The two walk together back down the hallway.

E–A–S–E Conversation Phases

PHASE 2: ASK — Small Talk

A   GUIDELINES / INSTRUCTIONS

- Small talk is transitional conversation that lasts for only a few minutes. It allows for 2 people to have a light-hearted conversation before they begin the "real" conversation.
- Be ready to make observations about the weather, your transportation, the décor of the office.
- Your networking contact will usually initiate small talk. But if your contact is socially introverted, you may need to start. It can be as easy as, "This is a beautiful building. Has the office been here for a long time?"

B   CULTURAL CUES

Knowing small talk is particularly important for client-facing industries such as consulting or investment banking, where you will be meeting with clients as part of your job. It's your job to make your clients feel comfortable and welcomed when they come to your office.

DO's

- Small talk is a sign of professionalism in the United States. Knowing how to do small talk is as important as dressing well.
- Small talk crosses social, political, and professional hierarchy. People do small talk when they get on the bus, when they go shopping, when they are in business meetings, and when they are at formal affairs.
- Across the U.S., certain regions are more likely to engage in small talk (Midwest, South) than in others (Northeast). Thus, in Texas, small talk is an important part of being socially graceful in everyday life while in NYC, people may not make small talk on the streets with strangers (they'll think you're weird!). However, in business settings, small talk is a must.

DON'T's

- Ask questions that are too personal, such as if they are married or have children. Stick with topics that are safe and lighthearted.
- Initiate conversation related to career advice. Hold off on that until you sit down and start the formal conversation.

C CASE STUDY / LANGUAGE EXAMPLES

Sample Small Talk & Opening

As Arjun and Ms. Riley are walking down the corridor:

Ms. Riley: How was it getting here?

Arjun: Actually everything went very smoothly. The plane was on time. Even the security line moved very quickly. Sometimes it can take awhile. Do you travel often?

Ms. Riley: Yes, about every other week, so I'm very familiar with the whole routine. I think I even know some of the TSA agents! So are you living on campus?

Arjun: Unfortunately I'm not. Housing is pretty tight for graduate students. But I live only 10 minutes from campus by bus. If the weather permits, I actually ride my bike to school. Good to get some exercise in.

Ms. Riley: Great idea. Well here's the office. Have a seat.

Arjun: Thank you.

Ms. Riley: So, Arjun, how can I help you today?

E–A–S–E Conversation Phases

PHASE 2: ASK — Opening

A   GUIDELINES / INSTRUCTIONS

- The formal conversation starts here, after the small talk ends.
- The Opening phase usually starts with a question from the networking contact. (S)he will ask questions such as: How can I help you? Tell me how things are going?
- Your objective is to set the tone of the meeting by your response. Tell him/her what you are hoping to get out of the conversation (remember, you're selling, so state your objectives appropriately).
- Provide an "overview" or yourself. This is where you tell your Core Story (30-second pitch / headline).

B   CULTURAL CUES

The switch from Small Talk to Opening can feel very abrupt if you're not used to it. You'll be talking about the weather and suddenly, the other person will ask you how (s)he can help you.

DO's

- Watch for non-verbal cues: your contact may pause for a second and look away, indicating the start of the next phase. It may be verbal cues: She may say, "so..." or "well, it's good to have you here..."
- Be ready with your objective and your core story. You want to be smooth and confident when you launch into the conversation.

DON'Ts

- Be unprepared to explain your objective or have your opening introduction ready. Networking contacts would find that as a sign that you are poorly prepared.
- Use phrases such as "refer me to a job" or "contacts who can help me find an internship." In the initial meeting, there should be no specific mention of the "job/internship." We all know why you're there. But our "game" is to talk about "career interests / career paths." It's too early for the contact to know if you are qualified or if they can help you. You don't ever want to put your contact in an embarrassing or awkward situation of having to say yes/no to a job opportunity.

C CASE STUDY / LANGUAGE EXAMPLES

ASK — Opening

Ms. Riley: (Finishing up small talk) Yes, I've been back on campus recently and it looks more beautiful than ever. I like the new building they're putting up. LONG PAUSE.

So...Arjun, how can I help you?

Arjun: Well, Ms. Riley, I decided to go to business school because I wanted to move into corporate finance, after having had 3 years of experience as a manufacturing engineer. Knowing that your background was in mathematics before coming to business school, I wanted to learn from you how you made your career switch. Also, I'm curious to learn why you chose corporate finance and how your role in corporate finance has changed during these years.

In my 3 years as a manufacturing process engineer at a bottling plant, I enjoyed the operations side, working with suppliers, the foreman, line workers, and the finance manager. I was energized to know that my management of suppliers and workers affected costs and therefore the profits of the company. While I enjoyed the problem solving aspects of engineering, I found myself drawn to the business side of things.

Ms. Riley: Arjun, please call me Susan. I'd be happy to talk about my career transition and my path in corporate finance. I'm curious why you're interested in corporate finance, when you could be doing venture capital or investment banking?

Arjun: In the end, I'm a person who enjoys being part of an operation. I think it's the engineer in me, who likes to build things. I want to make products; I want to work with people to figure out solutions. And I enjoy the accountability of seeing the outcomes. I'm fascinated by all the financial variables — building a complex capital investment model would actually excite me.

Remember that having your career story is entirely different from telling your story. Storytelling is improved only through practice. It may feel very embarrassing, but go practice your storytelling with an advisor or a friend who can give you feedback. Even more weird, but effective, is to record yourself with your mobile device or tablet. It's so helpful to know what you sound like, from another person's point of view! You'll know if you're on target with your tone, your speed, your usage of English. Better to know than to go in to your networking meeting "blind." Be courageous! Practice, listen to yourself, get feedback and aspire to tell your story as best as you can. It's your future!

E–A–S–E Conversation Phases

PHASE 3: SEE-SAW — Learn

A   GUIDELINES / INSTRUCTIONS

- In every networking conversation, learning from your contact's experience is a key reason you're there. You want to know the career path of someone who has been successful in the field you want to enter.
- Listening is critical in networking. You want to understand the factors that make people in this career successful. You want to learn about the skill sets and personalities they require.
- When you can learn about your contact's interests and preferences, you can present aspects of yourself that align with theirs. Human beings want to find things in common with others. The more you can find things in common, the more appealing you will become to your contact.

B   CULTURAL CUES

DO's

- Respectfully and sincerely learn about what the path to success looks like. When you network in the U.S, there is an expectation that you truly want to learn from the experience of the person you're contacting.
- It's okay to have a notepad on which you will take notes. It's a sign that you're taking this seriously.

DON'T's

- Sell hard in your Opening. You're not at the point where you are proving yourself. That comes later. The Opening is the introductory portion, where you are mutually getting to know each other's history and intentions.
- Follow a rigid path of what you plan to say. Let the conversation flow. Even if you don't get to make your key points here, you still have other conversation phases to pitch. Best to establish a good conversation flow and personal rapport at this point.

C   CASE STUDY / LANGUAGE EXAMPLES

SEE-SAW — Learn

Ms. Riley: Arjun, please call me Susan. I'd be happy to talk about my career transition and my path in corporate finance. I'm curious why you're interested in corporate finance, when you could be doing venture capital or investment banking?

Arjun: In the end, I'm a person who enjoys being part of an operation. I think it's the engineer in me, who likes to build things. I want to make products; I want to work with people to figure out solutions. And I enjoy the accountability of seeing the outcomes. I'm fascinated by all the financial variables — building a complex capital investment model would actually excite me.

Susan, when I read your profile on LinkedIn, I was fascinated to see that you were a math teacher prior to going to business school. What prompted you to go to business school?

Susan: Yes, I was teaching high school math. What I enjoyed the most was applying math to real life situations. I kept on having my students enter into business competitions as a way to utilize their math skills in a practical way. The more I did it, the more I realized how much I enjoyed the math of business, which is finance. I also enjoyed making real things, so when I went to business school, I explored different functions within finance, and corporate finance resonated the most with me. I've done corporate finance with different industries over the last 15 years and I've enjoyed understanding businesses through the lens of finance.

Arjun: You've been in such diverse industries, from transport manufacturing to high tech products. How did you make these big jumps? What have you found to be in common? I would imagine at some point, the process of corporate finance spans across industries.

Susan: Part of the fun, Arjun, has been to operate in different industries. I like the problem solving aspects of finance. I like complex products and financing growth in these contexts. I like making "things." There's a lot of satisfaction, working with people across functions, to figure out how to make a product, a business actually work. And my job is to figure out the financing, the funding. My job is to help make the numbers work. I fundamentally enjoy problem solving through math, with people, toward making something.

So Arjun, what are you thinking? Why corporate finance for you? You haven't had much direct professional experience in this area.

Many students feel very uncomfortable "bragging" about themselves in front of someone who's not only a stranger, but a person of authority. To make it easier, remember that these very kind people, who have agreed to speak with you, want to help you. But the only way they can help you is if they know where you shine and what you hope to do. Rather than feel embarrassed, feel excited! Excited about what is possible. Excited that the person speaking to you can open a door to your dreams!

E–A–S–E Conversation Phases

PHASE 3: SEE-SAW — Showcase

A | GUIDELINES / INSTRUCTIONS

If your goal is to explore career options, it's important to help your contact understand your competencies (what you're good at), your passions (what you enjoy doing), career options you're considering, and why you're thinking about those options. You need to provide this information so your contact can brainstorm with you and provide you with suggestions. You're not "selling" toward a job opportunity, so be straightforward about your career aspirations, what you're unclear about, and questions you have in order to make a career decision. Being authentic will be most helpful.

If your goal is to find job opportunities, you will need to "sell" your fit with the industry / position / company. Your contact is determining if you have the right skills and qualities. They're deciding if they should 1) provide you with feedback only or 2) if they're ready to go to the next step and introduce you to their network / company for job opportunities in the future. The more you "fit" with their ideal candidate in their industry, the more likely they'll introduce you to people who can hire you. You must talk about the transferability of your capabilities and interests in order for them to assess you and direct you to appropriate opportunities.

- **Be ready to answer interview–like questions.** Networking meetings are really interviews. The key difference is networking meetings are open-ended with no job commitment but they can lead you to job opportunities if you sell yourself appropriately.

- **Showcasing your fit isn't just about talking about yourself.** Asking thoughtful, strategic questions is incredibly important. It shows how curious and analytical you are about an industry, a company, or a job.

- **Pivoting is a key strategy to talk about your positives.** When your contact talks about a topic related to your interest or capabilities, you can agree, build and pivot to your own story (see example in Showcase Case Study).

B CULTURAL CUES

DO's

- Networking is in a "social" context, so your conversation is not as rigid and formal as in an interview. It's truly a conversation.

- Regardless of the level of the networking contact, the context is more "relaxed and social." Think "socially graceful." If you come from a hierarchical culture (where students wouldn't converse with persons in authority), it'll be helpful to think of these contacts as "a friend of a friend," who is your social equal. This will help you act and talk in a more relaxed way. Remember, they're talking to you because they want to help you! You're not in a formal interview.

- Americans love talking to people who are genuinely excited. Dare to show your personality! When human beings are excited about what we talk about, we naturally move our hands, talk with greater tonal variation, and widen our eyes. Don't think about how to look excited, just be excited!

- Talk about what you're good at. American contacts expect to hear about this at a networking meeting. There is a fine line between arrogance and confidence. If you come from cultures where you just "don't talk about yourself," use this trick. Talk about how your skills / capabilities have *helped* other people or your organization. When you talk about how your actions *benefited* someone else, it'll feel less like bragging.

DON'T's

- Spend the entire meeting listening to your contact. You need to showcase your capabilities so they know how to help you!

- Go into a meeting without knowing your top 3 key selling points (your benefits / capabilities / skills) or your core story. Others can't help them if you don't set a direction for them.

- Go into a meeting without having practiced talking about your capabilities / skills / interests / benefits. Written words don't easily translate to spoken words, so practice is critical.

Everyday socializing with American classmates is the best way to become competent in network socializing. Go to non-academic, social events, volunteer in student activities. Find ways to socially and verbally engage with Americans. You need to get the "feel" of American socializing. Once you do, job search networking will feel much less intimidating and terrifying. Socializing is not only good for networking; it'll also give you a greater sense of belonging to your university community and the American culture. Isn't that a win–win?

E–A–S–E Conversation Phases

PHASE 3: SEE-SAW — Showcase

C   CASE STUDY / LANGUAGE EXAMPLES

SEE-SAW — Showcase

Ms. Riley is now" Susan", given she asked Arjun to call her "Susan".

Let's pick up from where the "SEE-SAW—Learn" dialogue left off:

Arjun: You've been in such diverse industries, from transport manufacturing to high tech products. How did you make these big jumps? What have you found to be in common? I would imagine at some point, the process of corporate finance spans across industries.

Susan: Part of the fun, Arjun, has been to operate in different industries. I like the problem solving aspects of finance. I like complex products and financing growth in these contexts. I like making "things." There's a lot of satisfaction, working with people across functions, to figure out how to make a product, a business actually work. And my job is to figure out the financing, the funding. My job is to help make the numbers work. I fundamentally enjoy problem solving through math, with people, toward making something.

So Arjun, what are you thinking? Why corporate finance for you? You haven't had much direct professional experience in this area.

Showcase Begins Here:

Arjun: When I look back at my life, I think I've always been curious about how things are made, how things fit together. I've always liked to put things together and take things apart. That's why I loved spending hours building airplane models and then creating my own models to build. Because I was good in math and science, my parents thought I should pursue engineering or the sciences in college. I actually enjoyed it very much.

C CASE STUDY / LANGUAGE EXAMPLES

SEE-SAW — Showcase *(continued)*

Arjun: As I mentioned earlier, I enjoyed engineering. Like you, I enjoy problem solving and knowing how things work *[this is pivoting: agreeing, building, telling your story]*. The more complex it was, the better. But it wasn't just the engineering that I liked. I liked working with my team of diverse people, because each person had a different way of looking at the problem. When we were working on developing a bottling process that would improve efficiency and cost, I wanted to understand the whole picture. How did the process and the costs affect the larger business? How would the process affect the way we worked as a team? I was naturally drawn to calculating the financial side of things. I truly enjoyed working with our plant manager and finance manager to understand bottling from a business perspective.

That's why I came to business school. I enjoy the numbers. I like the idea of financing major projects. I like working with a diverse team and mediating through different points of view. I like to be at the point where the action and results take place. I'm still an engineer. I like making and creating stuff. Working with people, in a manufacturing environment, is where I see myself. So while I haven't had a finance job, I've been very close to it in my previous work. And I'm enjoying my finance class right now. I feel confident I can integrate very quickly into the finance function. I'm actually really looking forward to the opportunity to bring it all together.

Susan: That's really helpful and illustrative Arjun. I have a better understanding of what motivates you and what you're looking for. If you had an ideal industry to start in, what would it be?

...the conversation continues with more questions back and forth, the "SEE-SAW" continues.

Arjun's objective at this point is to

1) Understand the intent of Susan's questions

2) Find opportunities to establish point of competence, confidence and commonality by using the method I mentioned before: Agree, Build, Pivot to You

3) Engage in a natural, "see-saw" back and forth conversation.

E–A–S–E Conversation Phases

PHASE 3: SEE-SAW — Ask

A	GUIDELINES / INSTRUCTIONS

- It's important that you know your ultimate objective when you have your one-on-one conversation with a networking contact. Is it to learn about the industry? To get feedback about your readiness? To learn how to enter into the industry? To meet more people who can help you find a job?

- You may not get to the question you want to ask immediately. You may need to sell yourself first, learn about your contact's interests and perspective and/or maintain the conversation, before you have the chance. Patience, observation and appropriate timing can make all the difference. Remember, this is a conversation, not a Q&A period, so your social etiquette is extremely important. Social grace will be key to your success.

B   CULTURAL CUES

DO's

- Follow American social etiquette. What you want and how you ask are two different things. It's critically important that you follow appropriate American networking etiquette when you ask your questions.

- Practice how to ask what you want to know. Test it with your advisors, with Americans to see if it will be perceived appropriately.

DON'Ts

- Never ask for a job or internship in your first meeting. It's simply inappropriate. You may end the relationship right there, if the question is asked. American contacts know why you're meeting with them — to find a job! But they need to learn about you, decide if you're a good fit, before they'll feel comfortable introducing you. You need to prove yourself before you can ask for a job opportunity.

- Shoot questions one after another, to your contact. Again, this is a conversation, so think strategically when a particular question is appropriate to be asked.

- Never put your networking contact in an awkward situation. Don't force them to judge you and tell you right then and there if you can qualify for a job. Students have asked inappropriately, "Do you think I'm ready to have a job in this industry?" A better way would be to ask, "How do you think I could be best positioned to succeed in this industry?" Open-ended questions allow your contact to save face. Your contact may not think you're ready, but wants to be graceful in letting you know. Make sure you know how to "read between the lines." In other words, listen carefully to what they're trying to convey. It may not be literal and explicit.

E–A–S–E Conversation Phases

PHASE 3: SEE-SAW — Ask

C CASE STUDY / LANGUAGE EXAMPLES

SHOWCASE — Ask

Arjun: I've really enjoyed learning about your career path. I get really excited about how many turns you've taken in your career. Yet the core of your career has been about your fascination with numbers and how numbers affect companies — the people and the decisions they make. I totally get that kind of curiosity.

You've given me insights on so many fronts. As we wrap up, I'd like to get your candid feedback — in terms of my marketability for a corporate finance role, such as a financial analyst? What would you consider to be my strengths? My weaknesses?

Susan: Sure Arjun. I've enjoyed talking to you. I think one of your greatest strengths is your enthusiasm. You seem truly interested in corporate finance. You seem to really know what a financial analyst would be doing in a company, and that's really important. You sound like "an insider" even though you've never been in finance. I think your other strength is your related skills. Though you were an engineer, you have some of the fundamental analytical and quantitative skills required in finance. I'm glad to see you're taking finance classes. Doing well in those classes will be a proof of your competence, and create a good story to tell. I don't see any major weakness. Your lack of experience can be made up by your enthusiasm, knowledge of the daily work of a financial analyst, and more proof that you have skills that you can immediately use to help the business as a financial analyst. I would also think about industries you'd like to work in and why. Other than that, I think you're well positioned.

Arjun: Thank you Susan. That is wonderful to hear. It is so helpful to get your insights, on the positives and negatives, regarding my readiness. I'll make sure to think more about proof and industries I'd like to work in. In the meantime, if you know of other colleagues who have been switchers, like us, into corporate finance, I'd look forward to learning from them as well.

Susan: Let me think about that. There may be a few folks I'll put you in contact with. I think they'll enjoy meeting you too.

Arjun: Thanks so much, Susan. I'd love to talk to them.

E–A–S–E Conversation Phases

PHASE 4: END

A   GUIDELINES / INSTRUCTIONS

- Finishing with a summarized and graceful ending will validate your professionalism and maturity.
- Make sure to summarize key learning points you received from the conversation.
- Thank them for their advice and explicitly talk about what steps you'll take to utilize their advice.
- State your hope to keep in touch.
- Gracefully extend your handshake to end the conversation, saying, "Thank you so much for your time today."

B   CULTURAL CUES

DO's

- Maintain your professionalism all the way to the end! This means taking the time to thank them for their advice and to provide specific examples of what you've learned.
- These conversations end with a gracious handshake and expression of gratitude.

DON'Ts

- Feel you can end as soon as you get the information you want. Make sure you close the conversation professionally.
- Begin to show your disappointment or disengage when you realize this contact can't help you. Maintain your engagement and professionalism at all times, even if you feel this is not the best use of your time.
- Explicitly ask for a job in your first meeting. Make sure to use appropriate language.

American contacts want to be encouraging when these meetings end. It may be difficult to know "how you did." When a contact says, "please keep in touch," it may not mean that they think you're ready to interview, but it also may mean you did great! But here, Susan did say a couple of times, that she thought Arjun was in "good shape," which is a good implicit endorsement. The best way to know is to keep in touch with your contact and see how your communications proceed.

E–A–S–E Conversation Phases

PHASE 4: END

C CASE STUDY / LANGUAGE EXAMPLES

END — Bringing the Conversation to a Close

Susan: Well Arjun, thank you for coming to my office today. I'm glad to learn about your interest in corporate finance. I think you're in good shape, in general. Just need to address the areas I mentioned. Again, I think your enthusiasm plus your skills will make you a strong candidate.

Arjun: Thank you so much for your time, for sharing your history, and imparting your insights and advice into my career growth. I've learned that transition from another industry is possible with a combination of enthusiasm, knowing the actual work that needs to be done and with proven skills that I can bring to an organization. I look forward to learning from other colleagues that have switched from other industries as well. Thanks Susan (extending his hand for a handshake). I really appreciate our conversation.

Susan: My pleasure Arjun. I'll take a look to see which colleagues would be good references for you. Please keep in touch and let me know how things are going.

3) Follow-Up After Your Meeting

Thank You Note after your Meeting

A thank you note to your networking contact is part of American professional etiquette. It's a helpful way to summarize what you learned from your contact and to suggest keeping in touch with your contact. It's most helpful to send it within 24-48 hours of your meeting.

A   GUIDELINES / INSTRUCTIONS

- You can send a notecard and/or an email to your contact.
- A note card size is typically 3.5" x 5". It's best to use a design that is business-like and sophisticated. A well-known brand is Cranes.
- Notecards are most appropriate for more traditional industries like banking, consulting, manufacturing and non-profits. It is also expected from contacts who are 40+ years old.
- An email is most appropriate for high tech / start up companies.

B   CULTURAL CUES

DO's

- Address cards appropriately: date on top right (September 25, 2015) and salutation on next line, left justified (Dear Ms. Riley,).
- Write on the bottom half of the notecard first and then move to the top of the card if needed. Your content should not continue to the back of the card.
- Notecard content is going to be much shorter than what you'd write in an email, so you'll need to summarize your key points in 1-2 sentences.
- The email format is similar to that of the cover letter.

DON'Ts

- Write a novel! Keep it short and focused.
- This is not the time to be direct about jobs. It's a thank you plus a quick summary of what you gained from meeting your contact.

E–A–S–E Conversation Phases

PHASE 4: END

 CASE STUDY / LANGUAGE EXAMPLES

Thank You Note after your Meeting: Notecard

September 29, 2015

Dear Susan,

Thank you so much for meeting with me yesterday. I was encouraged to know that you successfully transitioned from a teaching career and I related it to your love for solving complex problems. Our conversation definitely confirmed my interest in corporate finance. I look forward to staying in touch. Thank you again for your time.

Best regards,

Arjun

C CASE STUDY / LANGUAGE EXAMPLES

Thank You Note after your Meeting: Email

Dear Susan,

I want to thank you for the time you spent with me yesterday. I truly appreciated learning about your career path, as well as your insights about your career in corporate finance.

Your path resonated with me — how you discovered an interest in corporate finance after you had chosen another career — yet some of the fundamentals remained constant. Like you, I have always enjoyed math and solving complex problems. As an engineer, constructing things, particularly with other people, has always motivated me. I really do think corporate finance will be a good fit for me.

I will continue to research this area as you suggested, especially the publications you recommended I read. I look forward to meeting with your colleagues. Thank you in advance for introducing them to me.

I will surely stay in touch throughout the year and I look forward to your continued counsel as the year progresses.

Best regards,

Arjun

4) Maintaining Your Relationships with Your Networking Contacts.

Networking is really about establishing and maintaining relationships. Some networking contacts are strictly for job opportunities, such as recruiters you meet at a career fair. Other contacts are teachers and mentors who have spent time with you, sharing their experiences to help you explore career options. Then there are the contacts with whom you really connected, who can become advocates and introduce you to job opportunities and interviews.

You can't know ahead of time which contacts will yield what outcomes. Your approach to networking should be as a "seeder" — planting seeds in many places. If you plant enough seeds, some of them will sprout! But you have to keep watering the plants to know which will yield fruit. Some may not, but you should expect that to happen. In fact, many of the initial emails you send may never get a reply. That's okay! Your objective is not to hit 100% response — that would be unrealistic. If you can get 20% reply on your initial emails, that's actually quite good! The response rate will differ for each student. The most important thing to remember is to keep trying.

So how do you "water" your seeds? How do you maintain your relationship so that at some point you can ask about job opportunities?

Here are some ideas:

1) Send an email when you've followed through on a piece of advice

Let's say Arjun reads some new magazines suggested by Susan. He finds a very interesting article that relates to his conversation with Susan. He can send her an email to let Susan know that he did read the publications. He can attach the thought-provoking article and share it with her.

Networking contacts like to know that the time they spent with you was worth it. So if you let them know you actually followed through on a recommendation, they'll appreciate it.

2) Let them know if you speak to a colleague suggested by your contact

You can let your contact know that you spoke to "Javier." Do a quick summary of the conversation and thank your contact for making the introduction.

This is also helpful because your networking contact may check in with Javier to see how the conversation went. If it went well, you may have developed another advocate. The more advocates you have, the more job opportunities you'll likely have as well!

) Send class-related articles / case studies

Remember, you're now on the cutting edge of your field. If you read a great article or case that your networking contact would be interested n, send it to her. You can provide a quick summary about the article case study and explain why you thought this article would be of nterest to your contact. Your contact will be impressed that you emembered your conversation and what matters to her.

) Send holiday cards

Americans tend to send cards at the end of the year given our elebration of Christmas / Hanukkah and at the beginning of the year or New Year's celebration. This is a great time to send a card to wish er a "Happy Holidays" and a quick update about you.

Note: If you decide to send an end-of-year holiday card, make sure to end cards that do not have Christmas trees on them. Do you know vhy? Christmas trees are a symbol of Christianity. There are many ndividuals who are not Christian, so be sure to send cards that say Holiday Greetings" but don't have a tree on the card. If you're not ure, then send New Year's cards. You can't go wrong with that!

Making The Ask For an Internship / Job

Let's say you met with a contact 2 months after school started and now t's time in the year for interviews for internships / jobs. What do you lo? Whom do you contact?

f you've maintained communications with your contacts *and* you have gotten positive and encouraging responses from them, then this is the ime to "harvest" your seeding, watering, and nurturing.

How do you know who would really help you? There's no easy answer o that question! It's about human connections so there's no formula. However, you always have indicators of their interest. Some may only want to be mentors while others are eager to be your advocates. Advocates tend to ask that you stay in touch, or offer to help you when you're thinking about finding a job. They tend to write back with tatements such as:

.. Please keep me updated as the year progresses.

.. Let me know when I can offer more support.

. I'd be happy to talk more in a few months when you're thinking about interviews.

. I'm impressed by what you've done so far and I think you'll be a really good fit for this industry.

.. Make sure you contact me when recruiting season happens.

International students often ask if keeping in touch, as I suggested to the left, would seem too aggressive. Absolutely not! For those of us who help students, we love to know the progress they've made or what's happening with them. These communications prove your ability to be relationship-oriented. That's an essential business skill. Be genuine in your interest in giving updates or sharing an exciting piece of news. We'll share in your excitement!

The art of networking is to be socially polite, maintain contact and when the time is right, do the "ask" in an appropriate manner! Asking is hard because you may get rejected. But if you never ask, you'll never know!

A   GUIDELINES / INSTRUCTIONS

- Send an email a couple of months before recruiting / interviewing will occur.
- You can follow the same process for making contact that was stated earlier in the book. However, you may decrease the repeats to only 2 times because you've already established a relationship and asking 4 times would seem too pushy.
- Make sure you provide a good reason for support. Tell them about the classes you've taken that have made you more prepared. Tell them if you earned good grades. Tell them about consulting / school projects that provided you with real life experience (especially if you haven't had much work experience prior to school).

B   CULTURAL CUES

DO's

- Use the same email format as with your initial contact.
- Follow up as suggested earlier in the book, but only repeat two times.
- Maintain a "professional" voice, even though you've developed a deeper relationship.

DON'Ts

- Expect to get an immediate response if you haven't kept in touch over the months.
- Use casual words, "wanna, gonna" or start an email with "Hey there."
- Refer to a specific job / title you saw on a job board, etc., as a start to your "ask."

C CASE STUDY / LANGUAGE EXAMPLES

Maintaining The Ask: Email

Dear Susan,

I hope this finds you well. I'd like to thank you for all the advice and insights you've given me over the last four months. I've gained such a practical understanding of corporate finance and its role in different industries. As you know, I've enjoyed my finance and strategy classes and I'm ecstatic that I did well in all of them.

At this time, we're entering into our recruiting season, and I'm hoping to get your counsel on ways to position myself for success. If you know of any job openings that would be a fit for my interests and skills, I would be most appreciative to learn about them. Would you have some time to talk in the next couple of weeks?

Many thanks in advance and I look forward to speaking with you!

Best regards,

Arjun

n Closing: Key Factors for Networking Success for nternational Students

Networking is about establishing a relationship

t is not transactional. You must convey credibility, trust and likability n order to succeed. People want to know you are competent, rustworthy and professional before they will connect you to people vho can help you find a job. That's why we never "ask for a job" when ve first meet someone. It may feel transactional to you, because Americans ask for help from people outside of their network, which is ot done in many countries. But be advised that we are still care about elationships!

See Networking as an interview, masked in social conversation

Understand that your contact is assessing your "fit". It's just like an nterview! They want to test you out before recommending you speak vith a colleague. Remember, how you "show up" with their colleague vill affect their reputation. So they need to assess you first!

nformational interviews, which are intended for exploring possible obs and careers, can be more of an "honest conversation". However, f you're speaking to someone who can help you enter a new career, 'ou're still "pitching" to that person! You're still selling.

Talk like an insider

f you do sufficient research, you'll learn about industry trends and argon/vocabulary so that when you meet with your contact, you'll ound like one of them! Contacts prefer to talk to individuals who are vell-versed in their area of specialty. They'll also be more impressed. And thus, more likely to recommend you to opportunities.

Understand pivotal networking and professional etiquette

t's such a shame when students, who mean well, end up sabotaging heir success because they violated an etiquette that is widely known to Americans. Aside from reading pointers from this book, make sure you ask and get feedback from advisors and American students. It's so understandable that you wouldn't know. But if you get advice and feedback, you'll feel more confident when you're out there networking

Stay focused and engaged even if you get a lot of rejection

Rejection is never easy! Never. Even for those of us who have networked a lot more. The individuals who have been successful are so incredibly focused. They're unbelievably savvy and brave. They embrace honest feedback and adjust their approach. They tweak their stories and improve their interpersonal engagement so they appeal more to potential contacts. They keep trying, even in the face of ongoing "no's". It's not easy. I admire all the students who try so tirelessly and persistently; they are my heroes.

Remember what a gift you are

Networking makes us feel vulnerable. Most of us are out there, asking for help and getting rejected more often than not. We can forget, in the middle of this thing called "networking", that everyone has a gift to give to the world. Each of us has competency that can help an employer. Each of us has a job waiting for us somewhere!

Learning to navigate effectively in the American culture can be so challenging! The American preference for individualism and personal storytelling can feel so boastful and uncomfortable for many. Even more so, asking "strangers" for help or for a job, is beyond comprehension for many international students! My point is…it can b uncomfortable. It should feel uncomfortable. You're in a new culture!

However, if you recognize your skills and talents and if you understanc what Americans care about, then telling stories about yourself will feel less awkward. If you dare to expand your identity to include American behaviors and are willing to practice and get feedback, you'll adapt more successfully.

Networking is one of the most complex job search skills! So be patient with yourself as you try this new behavior. It'll take some time to get used to it.

Most importantly, always remember that you are capable and knowledgeable. You are a gift to the world. There is a job out there that is perfect for you. Networking is but one method to get you there.

Good luck!